Silent Meow by T.K. Torme

The bonus of cats
is they will not ever bark.
Cats do rule the world.

~*T K Torme*

excerpt from pg. 80

Silent Meow by T.K. Torme
ALSO, BY T K TORME

In Conversation Vol 1 (Silver Bow Publishing)
In Conversation Vol 2 (Silver Bow Publishing)
In Conversation Vol 3 (Silver Bow Publishing)
In Conversation Vol 4 (Silver Bow Publishing)
Ite Missa Est Vol 1 (Silver Bow Publishing)
Ite Missa Est Vol 2 (Silver Bow Publishing)

Silent Meow by T.K. Torme

Silent Meow

by
T K Torme

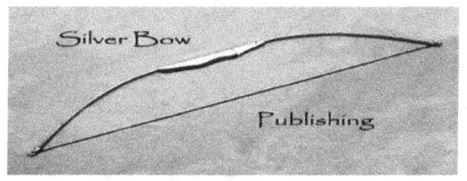

Silver Bow Publishing
720 Sixth Street, Box # 5
New Westminster BC CANADA

Silent Meow by T.K. Torme

Title: Silent Meow
Author: T K Torme
Cover Art : 'Pegasus Horse' painting by Candice James
Layout & Design: Candice James
Editing: Candice James

All rights reserved including the right to reproduce or translate this book or any portions thereof in any form without the permission of the publisher Except for the use of short passages for review purposes no part of this book may be reproduced in part or in whole or transmitted in any form or by any means either by means electronically or mechanically including photocopying recording or any information or storage retrieval system without prior permission in writing from the publisher or a license from the Canadian Copyright Collective Agency (Access Copyright)

Wwwsilverbowpublishing.com
info@silverbowpublishing.com
ISBN: 978-1-77403-341-8 paperback
ISBN: 978-1-77403 342-5 electronic book
© Silver Bow Publishing 2025

Library and Archives Canada Cataloguing in Publication

Title: Silent meow / by T K Torme.
Names: Torme, T. K., 1977- author
Identifiers: Canadiana (print) 20250125277 | Canadiana (ebook) 20250125285 | ISBN 9781774033418
 (softcover) | ISBN 9781774033425 (Kindle)
Subjects: LCGFT: Poetry.
Classification: LCC PS8639.O79 S55 2025 | DDC C811/.6—dc23

Foreword

This book is written by a person with Autism and Asperger's Syndrome. It is written openly and honestly through the mediums of memoir and insight. It gives the reader an in-depth glimpse into the feelings and emotions experienced by a person with a disability trying to navigate their way through a world of people without special needs.

Most times, people in general, don't bother to take the time to have meaningful contact with or get to know a person who is "different" from the norm in their social interactions.

It is difficult enough for people on the Autism spectrum, whether high functioning of not, to wend their way through this world's intricacies and nuances and find meaningful relationships.

A person with Autism has aspirations, wants, needs, and desires like any human being has. I hope after reading this book of insightful poetry the reader will have a greater understanding of what Autistic people feel deep inside their heart and soul.

Take the time to hear their "silent meow". ~ *Candice James, Poet Laureate Emerita, New Westminster, BC CANADA*

Silent Meow by T.K. Torme

This book is dedicated to the following people:

Candice James
whose editing of my book made the words shine.

Isabella Mori and Margo Lamont
who have been super supportive of my writing.

St. Scholastica my patron saint
St. Scholastica, please watch over me.

CONTENTS

Look Into My Aspie Self / 11
Angel / Noise / 13
Asperger Poem / 14
Blockage Of Emotions And Tears / 16
Chaos / 18
Emotions / 19
Friendship / 20
Funeral Vision / 21
I'm Locked In My World / 24
Invalidation Of And Emotions / 25
Invitation / 28
Marriage Dream / 31
Me / 33
Me, Myself And I / 35
My Best Friend / 36
My Heart / 39
Worlds / 41
You Do Not See Me / 42
You Don't Get / 44
Barbie Van / 46
Ottawa Chess Trip / 47
330 Grosvenor / 48
434 Strathcona / 49
Arrow / 51
Beat / 52
Bigfoot / 54
Cancer Woman, Scorpio Man / 56

Cats / 58
Choir / 60
Ski Chantecler / 61
Check / 63
Chores / 65
Christmas At 14 Kuhl Ave. / 66
Church Time / 70
Coffee / 72
Crows / 75
Épouse Inconnue / 77
Story In A Dozen Haiku / 79
Haunted / 81
Hell / 82
I Am / 83
Indiana Jones / 84
Inspiration / 85
Journal / 86
KGB / 87
Kindle / 89
Leonard Cohen / 90
List Poem / 92
Loss / 93
Pink Bunnies / 94
Salad Days / 95
Seagulls / 96
Sisters / 97
Battle Of The Brians / 98
The Seashore / 100
Tiger / 101
Unmasked / 102

Silent Meow by T.K. Torme

Weeping Willow / 103
When I Die / 104
Wild Cat / 105
Wonder / 106
Graveyard / 107
Whale Watching / 108
Roslyn Choir / 109
Ugunskurs / 110
Corner Talk / 111
November Sonnet / 112
Walking Stick / 113
Father's Day 1991 / 114
Annie / 115
Wasaga Beach / 116
Reward / 117
Pensionnaire / 118
Grade One / 119
Pink Boots / 120
MacDoherty's / 121
English Class / 122
Westmount Library / 123
Yann Hradecky / 124
Leo / 125

Author Profile / 127

Silent Meow by T.K. Torme

Silent Meow by T.K. Torme
Look Into My Aspie Self

I look deep into myself
and see all the books on the shelf.
I see different faces of my inner soul
as I empty the cherry bowl.

Life is more than staying within your inner shell.
You have to venture out if you want to stay well.

So I try to grow and blossom like a flower
and through this I get much more power.

By making connections I feel better about me
and that is always the best way to be.

Though Aspergers may take over my life
I try not to make it feel such a strife,
Aspergers gives me a sense of identity
and gives me such great liberty.

Each book on the shelf holds facts of my past
which I proudly display like a sailor's mast.
To learn from my mistakes is what I yearn for
so I don't become the world's biggest bore.

Bright colors may drive me insane
but I try not to go off to the side lane.
The smell of perfume may make me sick
but I've got the srength of a candlewick.

Silent Meow by T.K. Torme

It's better to go out and do things on your own
than staying at home, being quite alone

Friends are hidden where you see them not.
True ones are people who cannot be bought.

A sense of Aspie pride deep within me,
makes Aspergers seem the best way to be.

Silent Meow by T.K. Torme

Anger/Noise

Soft! How doth the noise of people
creep up upon my assaulted ears?
Ho, I wish I could drown them out forevermore.
Anger wells inside me like an abandoned pup
and I want to scream out at the world!
But yet I must frown
and deal with the world in a mask.

Little things,
like an out of place cup, drive me madder
than a nest of angry hornets.
If only I had a pair of wings
to soar free like an eagle in the sky.

I'd escape into a cave to hide
from all the noises of the world.

And yet I must come out of my shell
before a wave of anxiety comes over me.
Like a kitten curled up in a ball
I retreat into myself again and again.

Noise. Noise, so loud, all around me.
How I wish I were in a flock of bees!

Silent Meow by T.K. Torme

Asperger Poem

It seems other people don't care
that Aspergers is everywhere.

People who just don't seem to fit in
are told they belong in a trash bin.

My brain works differently from yours.
We both take different, separate doors

Sounds are much louder for me.
Babies crying is far from ecstasy!

Textures, tastes wreak havoc with my system.
Sounds you tolerate-torture me when I listen.

Making friends is a pure mystery for me.
It's like figuring out the birds and the bees.

Aspergers takes over my life.
I've been cut into two with a sharp knife.

Sometimes I'm good and know how to behave;
but at times my other half takes over-in a wave.

Sometimes I'm quiet and calm as a squire.
Other times I rage like an out-of-control fire.

Insignificant actions, gestures and words

Silent Meow by T.K. Torme
will make me angrier than a flock of wild birds

Aspergers ... I sometimes wonder-why me?
Yet this is the best way for me to be.

Silent Meow by T.K. Torme
Blockage Of Emotions And Tears

Blocked feelings and blocked words
are like a flock of caged birds.

I can't get my emotions out all straight.
They're stuck behind this blasted gate.

Feelings are all churned up inside of me.
I feel like an exploding African wild bee!

My autistic senses get messages mixed up.
I feel like an empty yet filled up full cup.

Why can't I cry like the rest of the world
instead of keeping my tears tightly furled?

Somehow I can't get the emotions just right.
Even when I try hard with all of my might.

I laugh at times when I'm supposed to cry.
When I should be sad-I'm not-and wonder why.

My mouth smiles while tears fill my eyes
and why's it so hard to say tearful goodbyes?

Why, why, why are my feelings so screwed?
I'd like myself to be whole and renewed.

Silent Meow by T.K. Torme

Blocked words, blocked feelings and fear.
And why do I shed an inappropriate tear?

I get past the point and can't cry anymore.
My tears are behind a heavy locked door!

My emotions, my emotions, are all blocked.
Will they forever be under key and lock?

Please help my autistic emotions be free
so I can become at last the real me.

Unblock my emotions so I'll be able to feel
what it's like to finally be steering the wheel.

To be able to go where I please and wish
and taste and savour every type of dish.

Autistic emotions don't have to be bound
and things that are lost can still be found.

And then when I'm able to finally cry free
It will help heal the inner-autistic me!

No blocked feelings, no more blocked words
will make me as free as a flock of wild birds!

Silent Meow by T.K. Torme

Chaos

A world filled with noise, lights, smells and touch.
People all around so attuned to themselves
expect me to know all of this - but it's too much
for me to handle. Forever I feel like an inept elf
who has to hustle and bustle
to keep up with the world.
I who cannot process the all-too-bright light
or the high-pitched noise of people.
get curled into a little ball-
closed far away from the world.
I try to recapture my sense of self
through books.

Give me time to process your information-
calm and slow.
I will get it with a chance
to sort the x's and o's.
I'll filter your ideas through my mind
and with time I know
I can find the answer
as I sort through this chaos.

Chaos, chaos,
and more chaos all around
I sometimes feel helpless
overwhelmed and snowbound!

Silent Meow by T.K. Torme

Emotions

I'm feeling sad, I'm feeling blue.
I cannot shake this feeling inside of me.
I don't know what's real, don't know what's true.
Am I you? Are you me? I'm confused as can be.

Constant criticism wherever I go.
I take it all in – I boil up inside.
I don't let it out – I'm about to blow!
Constant yellings by my peers
rob me of my fragile pride.

I cannot take it anymore – I just wanna die.
What's the use of saying how I really feel?
You'll dismiss me– with a wave of goodbye.
You treat me like a vehicle with a flat wheel.

I must not cry – or express my sadness.
To show my true emotions is not allowed.
No swearing, cussing, crying or loud laughing.
We must be aware of people passing.

I'm tired of keeping all my emotions in.
I wanna express 'em 'til I'm blue in the face.
I don't care if you throw me in the trash bin.
I'm human too – let me express "me" anyplace!

I don't care about what's right and what's wrong.
I'll get you to listen to me if I have to use a gong!!

Silent Meow by T.K. Torme

Friendship

Oh, friend, thou hast stood in the test of time
And been with me through trials and tribulations
Thou hast offended me with your awful rhyme
And put me into the depths of despair! Elations!
I'm rid of thee at last – that awful smell of yours
With your false friendship and your idol Gods.
I can seek new friends and find new doors
And achieve a higher value with a mere nods.
Thou hast done me great malice and harm
And cut me off in times of my great need.
Your cold words in my heart with ice did form.
You were cruel and selfish out of greed!
How can you say you are a friend to me
When you cut and wound my heart eternally?

Silent Meow by T.K. Torme
Funeral Vision

In my life I've made lots of friends
and have lots of family around me.
I've married well, have children
and grandchildren around me.
who love me very much.
It's a great support system I can count on
in times of great need.
People are always there for me –
no matter what.

As I get older I get sicker
and my entire support system
is there to rally around me –

Loads of visitors who travel from afar
just to see me when my health is failing,
lots of food pouring in by the carload –
no need to cook – just heat up and eat.
And people there to do the dishes
and clean up for me.

I feel loved, special, wanted and needed.
It feels great to have people there
who really care for me and I love it.
My funeral arrangements have been made
with the service I wanted.

My obituary has already been mostly written

Silent Meow by T.K. Torme

and ready for print in the major papers.
My will has been finalized
With explicit instructions for
the division of my belongings.
My tombstone is nearly ready
with the words I want on it.
I've dotted every single "I"
and crossed every single "T".
I'm prepared to die in peace.

When I die, everybody weeps and cries with
Sorrow. My friends and family are round me.
I take my last breaths. I have a lovely
funeral church service – I'm not religious, but
I love church funerals; they're so romantic.
The church overflows with people –
It's standing room only

And people come from round the world
to pay their last respects to me.
People cry and weep, a touching eulogy
is read and stories about me are told.
Some funny and some not.

The reception is crowded with people.
My favorite soft pink mini carnations
the main flowers–It's great.
But the real truth is – all of this is made up.
None of this is true. I don't have people like that
who care about me. There's nobody who will ever

Silent Meow by T.K. Torme

want to marry a freak like me –
unwanted and unloved –pushed away
by my own father who left me at age 3.

Nobody cares for rejects like me.
I'm constantly pushed away and ignored,
shut away from the light
where none can see me.

The real cold hard truth is
I'll probably die all alone
and nobody will even care
or notice I've gone.

Nobody will ever bother to come
to pay their last respects to me ...
       because I don't matter
               to anybody.

Silent Meow by T.K. Torme
I'm Locked In My World

I'm locked in my world-
and I cannot get out.
I'm locked in my world-
and I wanna shout.

I cannot tell you how I really feel
as I'm locked in my world.
I feel like I'm in a banana peel.
I'm locked in my world.

My words are stuck in my throat.
All in a big jumble.
I'm locked behind this castle and moat
where I'm left to tumble and stumble.

I'm locked in my world
and I cannot cry.
I'm locked in my own world.
I just wanna die.

Why can't I run like the rest of you?
Why am I awkward in anything agile?
Locked in my world - don't know what to do.
I'm locked in my world-so very fragile.

Locked, locked, locked in my own world
Locked, locked, locked forever
in my autistic world.

Silent Meow by T.K. Torme
Invalidation Of Feelings And Emotions

I really do not know what to do anymore –
I'm at my breaking point.
I try to express how I really feel
but am slapped down instead.
If I cry or laugh too much –
I'm told to stop – Get me out of this joint!
I cannot express how I truly feel
without wishing I were dead.

Why must I live with someone
who is so cruel and cold;
someone who puts me down
at every turn I do or make,
I try my hardest to stand up again –
to become bold but that doesn't work –
I'm in for the final take.
Right now I wanna end my life –
get out of this torment.
If I cannot cry why am I living
on 'God's Green Earth'?

What is love? Can you tell me?
Or will you tell me to get bent?
I feel so very angry all the time
and am not given my wide berth!
I just want to be held and loved –
is that too much to ask?
To be held, cuddled, and stroked –

Silent Meow by T.K. Torme

to validate what I'm feeling.
It's not much to request –
just a small favor – are you up to the task?
I feel so unloved and unwanted these days –
you can peel me off the ceiling.

I'm being told what to do all the time –
this just isn't right.
How and who to be friends with
is suffocating my inner soul.
I'm treated like a child and I hate that –
I want to fight and fight! I hate it here I really do –
I'm like a big, empty bowl

I wanna break out of here to live out on my own
but I'm scared to do just that –
I don't even know how to survive at all.
How to pay bills, clean, cook –
all confusion – why not throw me a bone?
Help me to become free of all this abuse –
let me stand tall!
My house has no love or warmth here
only cold and sadness. I'm yelled at
all the time for things I don't even do.
I hate my life.
I want to be loved and hugged.
I really need to have constant gladness.
I need to be hugged and kissed –
tell me I'm loved –
do not split me in two with a knife.

Silent Meow by T.K. Torme

Hold me and tell me I will be ok
and everything will be fine
Validate my emotions – let me cry
on your shoulder, in your arms.
I need to express how I truly feel –
perhaps over a bottle of wine?
What I could truly use these days
are a couple good luck charms.

I'm going insane keeping my true feelings in.
Expressing them gets me
constant laughing and scorn.
I feel why bother anyway;
why not throw me into a trash bin?
Keeping these powerful emotions inside me
makes me feel forlorn and torn.

Silent Meow by T.K. Torme

Invitation

I'm well loved by
all friends and family.

Whether we're near
or far geographically,
we keep in touch frequently
by phone and by email.

You tell me everything that
goes on in your life –
births, sicknesses,
marriages, divorces, trips. And
because you know I'm not able to
make it to events, you still let
me know, no matter what, always
extending an invitation towards me.

You even go out of your way
to give me a ride to family reunions
so I can spend time with everybody.

When trips are planned,
You go out of your way to include me
and invite me along because you
really want to make sure I'm included and
have an awesome opportunity to travel
and get to know you better as a person.

Silent Meow by T.K. Torme

And because you know I'm financially challenged,
You make sure to go out of your way to help me
find a way to travel –
maybe an all expense paid trip–
because you are an awesome person.

You will go out of your way to ensure I come
To your wedding because I'm important to you.
You include me in everything, invite me along
because you want to make me feel included,
Loved, wanted, special. It's a great feeling
to be always invited, included,
and be told all that goes on in your lives –
I feel honored and touched.

But what I've just told you is
all a horrible bold-faced lie –

That's just not true in
My own personal life:

The real cold hard truth is a
Bitter pill to swallow – I don't have
anybody like that in my life –
everybody pushes me away,
treats me like I don't exist
or considers my feelings.

They probably don't think I have
feelings or even care that they don't

Silent Meow by T.K. Torme

share with me what's going on
in their lives or that they block my emails –

I'm the resident retard with a
'Disability' that can't do anything right.

The cold hard truth is this:
Nobody ever bothers to go out of their way
to invite me to events or include me on trips.

Because to them: I just simply don't exist.

Silent Meow by T.K. Torme

Marriage Dream

You and I had met.
We dated for years.

We're a serious couple.
We're living together you and I.

''I love you. You matter.''
You say that to me constantly.

We spend time with our families –
His parents like me/my mother

likes him – it's a beautiful blend,
melting, meshing of two families.

You propose to me in a romantic
way – beautiful, poignant. I accept.

We get married in a beautiful
simple ceremony. Both our

entire families come to the wedding.
Blessings from all. A great celebration.

We have two beautiful children –
a girl first, then a boy.

It's a great life we live together.

Silent Meow by T.K. Torme

We have a happy family, full of love.

The children are well behaved.
They're smart and talented

and well adjusted. They never
get into trouble, are polite

and kind and courteous. They
grow up and go on to do great
things with their lives. We're
A Norman Rockwell family.

But now back to present day,
the current reality when I realize

it's all a figment of my imagination
and will never happen to me.

Silent Meow by T.K. Torme

Me

I am not a person with a Barbie Doll Figure,
nor do I want to be.
I am someone who has strived to lose weight
through normal exercise and food intake.
I am round and plump but proud of it.
I do not wear makeup of any kind on my face,
nor will I ever do so except if forced to do so.
I seek for inner beauty
that is more important than outside looks.

I am not studious, a straight
"A" student, an honor roll person,
someone who wins countless awards
or can get any job with very little effort.
I 'm a "C" student at best, try hard to study
and have difficulty landing
even the most repulsive job
known to mankind: telemarketing.

I have never committed a crime,
never skipped school,
have always been obedient
to my teachers, been devoted to school.

I am not popular,
do not have many friends.
I struggle to keep the friends I have.
They are precious to me.

Silent Meow by T.K. Torme

I am just me:
Young, smart, poor, trying to survive
in a world of racism and hate.

I am not rich,
I do not have money to travel around the world,
I don't have a car, my clothing and shoes
are in rags, I am making ends meet.

I have not traveled much,
The most exotic country I've been to
is the United states, but I do desire
to travel the whole world in detail.

I am not racist.
I embrace people of all shapes, sizes, color.
I strive to understand every culture on earth.
I love all things great and small.

THIS IS ME:
TAKE IT OR LEAVE IT.

Silent Meow by T.K. Torme
Me, Myself, And I

When I was born, I knew
I would become eccentric
and nobody would like me.

By the age of twelve
I was already reading any
thick book I could get my hands on.

I hope, by the age of thirty,
I will become a contestant on Jeopardy.

Silent Meow by T.K. Torme

My Best Friend

We met you and I
when we were children
We really clicked you and I.
We really got along well
With each other. We had
lots of common interests.
We played together all
the time; dinner at each
other's houses, sleepovers
and even vacations together.

Both our families would spend
the holidays and birthdays
together, becoming a close-
knit stitched patchwork
quilted family.

We all get along together and when
we grow up we both want
to pursue the same career in
writing. We both get accepted
to the same University program
where we study and live together.
It's really great because
we help each other with our studies
and we both thrive together.

We have a symbiotic relationship you and I –

Silent Meow by T.K. Torme
A sighted horse leading the blind horse –

One cannot live without the other.
We are each other's seeing eye horse.

When we date, we look out for each other,
watching for that perfect potential
husband – We double date as much
as possible – and we all form an awesome,
wonderful cohesive relationship
between the four of us.
Our boyfriends propose at the same time
and we end up in having a double wedding –
Double the fun and cost effective.

We buy our wedding dresses together
and the day is awesome.
Our families and friends travel
from all over to celebrate the occasion.

After the wedding, we all honeymoon
Together – because we got a great deal.
The honeymoon is awesome – sightseeing
in out of the way places, seeing impressive
Historical sights, meeting new people,
eating strange and mysterious food,
relaxing, writing – it's great – all four of us
are writers so we understand each other
and we start to form a collaboration
on a series of writing projects.

Silent Meow by T.K. Torme

This is the start of an awesome, long
collaboration of writing together – our pact
to stick together – to write, to support –
as a team, a herd. We become successful
together – a large, cohesive family unit
Eventually we pool our resources to buy
a house together and share expenses.

We have a beautiful life together –
One, big, happy family. La vie est belle.

But this is only a fairy tale I've
Just told you – a horrible Grimm's tale.

The real truth is the mirror opposite:
I've never had any best friends like that
in my life – I never will. I never
grew up with a best friend since childhood
I will never have a friend like that –
Nobody is willing to be my best friend
like that – whatever "best" friends I've
had over the years were short and fast.
Blooming as a cactus flower in the desert.

They come and fade away eventually
as ghosts, sinking like the Titanic.
and then I'm left alone – a solitary insect.

The real, cold, hard truth is:
    I'll always be alone.

Silent Meow by T.K. Torme

My Heart

My heart is as wide
as the world's oceans

filled with millions
of pearls glistening

in the water's sunlight.
It's filled with gold

ready to shine
at a moment's notice.

My heart wishes to
be there for others

in time of need.
My heart is filled

with masked love
hidden underneath

a screaming heart.
Every single time I

offer to help out
of the goodness of

my heart, i'm met

Silent Meow by T.K. Torme
with venom, eroding

me away as a
sand washed beach,

stomped on 'til
eventually my heart

becomes as cold
and dark as a

black hole and
my voice becomes

as silent as a grain
of sand in the

Sahara Desert.

Silent Meow by T.K. Torme

Worlds

You and I live
in two separate different
worlds – separated by
an electric fence.

I want to join your
world – to know who
you are – to speak your language.

I knock on your door –
hoping you let me in.
Silence. I knock louder.

You open your window,
pelting me with acid –
yet I knock louder.

You throw sewage waste,
vomit and rotten food, hoping
I disappear like a mirage.

Your message – as clear as
ice freshly frozen in the
Winter's frost. I do not go away.

I only want to be part of
your world you so eagerly
keep me away from.

Silent Meow by T.K. Torme
You Do Not See Me

You do not see me
but I see you.
Through my shadows. I can be
whatever I wish – so I don't become blue

Through your mocking eyes of hate
you see me and my autism as a threat.
My handwriting amongst you has become debate –
Of whether or not you can read it – that's become a bet.

I walk, talk and act differently than you.
Can you comprehend me? Can you see into my soul?
I don't think so! I don't think so at all! This ''new''
Interpretation I have on the world –
like looking into a glass bowl.

How can you say you know me?
Why do you say that is true?
You say we should let things just be
like an old comfortable tennis shoe?

I hide in my autism world,
my private little place.
I see you much better than you see me.
I know you much better than you think.
Your face is ingrained into my soul –

Silent Meow by T.K. Torme

I just can't let things be.

Me, I'm smart – smarter than you think
I comprehend the world differently –
My solutions unique to the world – in a blink
of an eye – like seeing it through the TV!

You can't hurt me with your tauntings
nor with your bullying, mocking and jeers.
Remember I will come back to you with many
hauntings until you are brought to tears.

I can see you clearly now –
Can you see me too?
Nope you cannot with your baggage in tow.
I retreat into my world to escape being blue

You do not see me
But I see you.
Through my shadows I can be
whatever I wish
to escape from being blue.

Silent Meow by T.K. Torme
You Don't Get

You don't get to tell me
my arms are useless or
compare me with others.

you don't have the right
to put me down and
humiliate me as if
I'm some piece of filth.

I have a right to
make my own mistakes.
I can make my own choices
and decisions. I have
the right to change
and grow.

I deserve to be happy
and successful. I cannot
change the color of
my skin, my shoe size
or the fact I'm autistic.

Telling me to look
in a mirror before
I buy hot chocolate
or that my face is a fright
is hurtful and mean.

Silent Meow by T.K. Torme

You've yet to get
my magic, my talents,
my dreams and goals.

My unique combination
of gifts, talents and
abilities are my own
original symphony.

Silent Meow by T.K. Torme

Barbie Van

A Barbie Van with accessories
was casually, but carelessly,
purchased at a garage sale.

The toys came home,
shoved away
in a darkened corner
of my room – never to see
the light of day
while my books glittered
and shone in my room.

Cousin Zara came
to visit us in Montreal.

I "sold" her my set – by
Insisting she take it.
I would not let her leave
without the van
and ALL its accessories.

Silent Meow by T.K. Torme
Ottawa Chess Trip

In grade six I went to Ottawa
with my chess club for the day.
We visited the Science Center
where I bought a cool bookmark.

We played chess
with other students.

On the Rideau Canal
I walked in my boots
with one of the teachers –
enjoying the crisp, fresh
sunny winter day.

Then ...
a bus ride back to Montreal,

Silent Meow by T.K. Torme
330 Grosvenor

Moved to Grosvenor

Have new bed
Have new desk
Have new drawers
Have new everything

Clean, tidy room
My cat Cuddles
On my bed

Triple decker radio

Have breakfast
Brush my teeth

Get dressed in closet
Have no drapes

Good old
Salad Days.

Silent Meow by T.K. Torme
434 Strathcona

Do you remember
the Good Old Salad Days
Of Montreal?
You lived in 434
Strathcona – Westmount
Québec – where we both
roamed the Noble Halls
of Roslyn Elementary.
I lived with your family
in 1987 when my mother and I
lost all our belongings in
storage – that year of Hell.
Yet I went to church with
you – my inner peace of
God and comfort. We called
CJAD, talked to Santa –
The tape I still have.
The year I got my ears pierced.
Your mother's Christmas gift.
We played together, had
fun – trick or treating
in Westmount, sledding on
Park King George.
Memories in my mind –
Ghosts of a distant past.

Silent Meow by T.K. Torme
That most wonderful time
when my world turned
upside down – life in chaos
I'm growing up now in Vancouver, BC,
I still remember those
Good Old Salad Days
Of Montreal.

Silent Meow by T.K. Torme

Arrow

During the summer
at Deaumaine Deauville
I met you shortly
before my birthday
where I saw you sliding
down the slide into
the pool. We struck
A fast friendship where
we played nearly every
day – games of all sorts –
chess, computers,
archery etc. together.
We shot with your bow and arrows –
you with perfect precision.
And me who could
easily accidentally injure
or murder with my faulty aim.
Those lost arrows in the woods
are now my lost friendship with you
as we drifted apart after I moved
to BC in 1992.

I never forgot you.
And I remember you every
Year on your birthday
on November 4.
What happened to you?

Beat

Hear the rhythm
of the music.

Drums beating to
our battered souls.

Lips kissing in
a tango of

sweet chilled chocolate
pudding with whipped

cream while we
wear white masks

tango dancing our
damaged souls, ghosts

hidden betwixt us,
trying to send

mixed messages of
love and hatred.

Together you and
I slowly unmask

each other with

Silent Meow by T.K. Torme

words, gestures and

affection. We learn
to rock our

masks of hate
and of loathing -

We learn to
accept our true
selves behind the
onion layers masked

by perceptions of
who others want

us to be.
You and I

kill our last
ghost together while

we take our
Road Trip Orange
together.

.

Silent Meow by T.K. Torme

Bigfoot

Back during the good
Old Salad Days in Montreal
my mother took us to
Beaver lake.

A sunny spring day.
The apple crisp air
Upon our faces.

You spotted your friends
upon the muddy pond –
went up to talk to them.

In your snow-white shoes
you crossed the spring thaw
getting stuck on the way back

Molasses slow motion
walk-caked – blob
"The Thing" – creature.

A CBC crew filmed nearby.
You spotted them – became
upset and cried.

You were scared your mother
would see you with us on TV
with your dirty shoes.

Silent Meow by T.K. Torme

We took you to the nearest
bathroom to clean your shoes
and dry your tears.

I wonder after all those
years if your mother found
out. Do you still remember
that day too?

Silent Meow by T.K. Torme
Cancer Woman, Scorpio Man

Cancer woman, Scorpio man –
it's a combination worth trying –
it makes me a fan.
Cancer's moody ways can be
too much for others –
but not for the Scorpio man.

Moody, broody Cancer woman's
lashing negative way
perfect for Scorpio man's secretive way –
to keep it at bay.

Scorpio man can be faithful to those
he takes under his wing
but watch out for his sting –
should you have an extramarital fling.

As lovers in bed Scorpio and Cancer
are a perfect match – not to be beat.
Two people together – in unison –
under the covers together –
producing much heat.

Cancer woman can nag and complain
like a pro at work too
holding onto old pasts and hurts –
going over old thoughts anew.

Silent Meow by T.K. Torme

Scorpio man, too, with his secrets
and home making nature – like kin.
Deep underneath his outer shell –
his sensitive nature – under his skin.

Sss! Watch out! When Cancer woman
and Scorpio man produce a romance
dancing together, in unison – to get her –
always – at a glance.

Yes, more people should produce
a Cancer woman Scorpio man match.
It's a great combination – for both –
makes a great catch.

Cancer woman, Scorpio man –
together forever always true and good.
Cancer woman, Scorpio man – yes,
together like good wine and fine food.

Cancer woman, Scorpio man.

Silent Meow by T.K. Torme

Cats

I

Cats are cuddly, cute and annoying.
Cats are very playful-
when you least want them to be.
I say this because when you're doing your homework
all of a sudden a fur ball comes from nowhere and
sits innocently on the paper you are doing.
Cats will just purr for the sake of purring and
cats will sleep on your bed
and keep you company when
you are sick. All in all
cats are fun to be with-fur and fangs.

Cats

II

Cats, cats, cats.
You never see them near bats.
They like birds and mice and rats.
Always sleeping on mats.

Cats, cats, cats.
So cute and cuddly
and sometimes funny.
They're like acrobats.
Cats, cats, cats

Silent Meow by T.K. Torme

Cats

III

Flying fur,
a hiss, a howl and then a purr
as with one jump
a lump became
two cute cuddly cats,
not cunning creatures
who with a claw
protruding from the paw
draw a line across the veneer
of the table and the sheer
drapes dangling dizzily
in the breeze
of the open window.

Silent Meow by T.K. Torme

Choir

Back during the Good Old Salad Days
I walked the Noble Halls of Roslyn.

I was in the Roslyn school choir
with Mme. Gagne and Mme. Bryant –
Tuesdays and Thursdays at lunch -
choir rehearsals, music -
pure blissful peace for my heart.

The concerts. We went to, a radio recording
for CJAD's Children's Christmas choir songs.
Our treat after concerts was McDonalds
where I always had cheeseburger,
strawberry milkshake, and fries.
Times always remembered-
I kept all the songs we did for decades
until 2014 – and then
I paired them down to two songs
that meant the world to me –
'Memory', from 'Cats'
and our school song.

I still sing it to remember
the Good Old Salad Days
when I walked the Noble Halls
of Roslyn Elementary.

Silent Meow by T.K. Torme
Ski Chantecler

Back during the Good Old Salad Days
of Montreal my mother and I
spent many winter weekends
going downhill skiing.
She put me in ski school
To learn how to ski.

I was never stable on my feet
let alone two pieces
of wood that moved –
making me wobble off balance.

Yet, I spent many happy days
on the hill followed by
frog legs or escargot.
Delights I dream of
to this very day.

One weekend we went to Chantecler
For skiing and fun.
The day started fine:
ski downhill,
repeat all over again.

Until one dodgy ski lift –
too fast –
I missed the chair
going over the mountain rocks

Silent Meow by T.K. Torme

Tumbling
  all
  the
  way
  down
    in
    a
    snow
    ball
    to
    the
  bottom.

By God's grace I
 was only shaken up – not hurt –
angels most certainly must have protected
me from great harm.

I didn't realize it at the time
but over the years I've come to realize
God was watching over me that day
and I am truly grateful
For His protection.

That day is long gone
but I fondly recall that time
      during
The Good Old Salad Days
    of Montreal.

Silent Meow by T.K. Torme

Check

You never call
to talk to me.

You never email
just to say hello.

You never share
family news with me.

When you call
you never ask

to talk to me.
I'm only a ghost.

I pretend I'm fine.
I pretend I don't care.

I pretend all is cool
I pretend all is well.

I pretend I'm not mad.
I pretend I'm not angry.

I pretend I'm not hurt.
My feelings are fine.

IT'S A BOLD-FACED LIE.

Silent Meow by T.K. Torme

I'm not fine.

I do care.
All's not cool.

All's not well.
I am mad.

I am angry.
I am hurt.

I'm the ghost
you just ignore

while I choke
back acid tears,

mask my feelings
so you can

be my friend.
Are you my friend?

An illusion as
you never check

to see
how I'm doing.

Silent Meow by T.K. Torme

Chores *

Chores, chores, chores!
That is all I do!
If I close my doors on chores
I'd go to Timbuktu!
Chores, chores, chores!

****Originally written in 1984 – as a child –
the very first poem I ever wrote.***

Silent Meow by T.K. Torme
Christmas At 14 Kuhl Ave.

On Christmas Eve Santa always delivered
Christmas memories during supper.

Our family would gather 'round
the long oval table, the wafer
crisp tablecloth – white as
pure driven snow. The table –
always set with the Santa Advent
Candle which Opa carefully cleaned
each year after its yearlong slumber.

He put each candle in – with care –
as a surgeon performing the most
intricate brain surgery. I'd watch
with delight as the candles were
lit, waking Santa up for his yearly
exercise where we would delight
in watching Santa exercise while we
feasted on goose, sauerkraut and potatoes –

Goose as tender and soft as baby feathers.
Potatoes as golden as the Egyptian sun.
Sauerkraut melting in your mouth, not hands
'til we were as stuffed as a taxidermy animal –
unable to move. My Mother's family is Latvian –
My grandparents were Proud of their roots
and where they come from.

Silent Meow by T.K. Torme
I never learned to speak their language
save but a few words here and there – enough
to season my bare rudimentary grasp of
the language. They all spoke Latvian round
the dinner table and throughout the evening –
their own secret world and club only they
had the key to. I knocked several times,
trying to pound the door down,
but it was always built stronger
to keep me out of their conversations.
I slipped into my own world instead –
where only I had the password to my
own secret thoughts and words.

I'd make up private jokes, funny thoughts
and secret quizzes only I knew the answer to.

While we ate, I swore I heard a clatter on
the roof – not loud as thunder but soft
as feet crunching on hard snow. And
of course Uncle Moe would mention
Santa had come round for presents.
He'd get that twinkle in his eye – and

the entire family would delight in this
conversation 'til after dessert when
we'd slowly meander down to the basement
where the tall anorexic tree filled with
ornaments, tinsels and live candles stood –
as proud as a child on their first day of school

Silent Meow by T.K. Torme

The lit candles were of Christmas promises,
memories and old ghosts. Each person would
pick a candle and make a silent wish for future
dreams. The last candle lit was the winner
granted of a lottery – a game of chance.
But the actual lit tree was magic in itself
bringing you to a new magical world
where pink bunnies could be drawn at
your heart's desire if you wished.

Opa would play German Christmas songs
while we sat in front of the roaring fire.
We listened in silence while feasting on nuts
and oranges after our royal feast.
And then us children – Myself, Marta,
Amanda, Aina and Andra would perform
before we handed out the Christmas gifts to
the rest of the family. We took the presents
from under the tree which was bare before
our meal. When we went down after supper
a magical act of presents filled under the
tree for everybody. The performance of either
a song or poem was not what mattered.
It was the Latvian tradition –
carrying the memories
I have to, this very day,
of my entire family as one.

And remembering how Santa always

Silent Meow by T.K. Torme
delivered Christmas memories during
Christmas Eve supper to us ...
on 14 Kuhl Ave.

Silent Meow by T.K. Torme

Church Time

In the good Old Salad Days of Montreal –
We were children - best friends –
Melissa and I slept over
at each other's houses, telling ghost stories,
laughing late into the night, killing old ghosts.

On Sundays I'd go to Church with Rom and you –
Wesley's Anglican Church – songs of Faith
a place of warmth, safe belonging, wanted –
homilies of lessons to be learned –
Sunday school and God and Bible,
Normal family time – my "adopted" family.

"Papa" Rob, "Sister" Melissa –
secret family – no one knew –
not even you. Yours once
Gave me a small Happy Birthday Button –
I wore 'til words faded – memories still
strong in my mind.
You brought me your acceptance

You taught me conversations in candlelight
and classical music – that God was okay
to believe in – safe haven
with you and your father.
Being *listened* to, feeling
alive – grateful and thankful
for spending time with you.

Silent Meow by T.K. Torme

Remembering the Good Old Salad Days
of Montreal when we were children,
when there were no old ghosts to kill.

Do you or your father remember me ...
After all of these years?

Silent Meow by T.K. Torme

Coffee

I talk to people.
I'm not anti-social.

I enjoy meeting new people.
I enjoy making new friends.

I meet you randomly.
We talk for a while.

I'm interested in getting to know you better.
I'm interested in dating you.

Perhaps a normal relationship.
Boyfriend/girlfriend.

I'm like other people.
I want you to ask me out.

But the conversation ends
and we part ways.

Maybe we meet again or not.
But you never ask me out for coffee.

You are never interested in me.
You are interested in that other woman.

The prettier, thinner woman.

Silent Meow by T.K. Torme

The more athletic woman.

The socially acceptable woman.
The woman with pleasant conversations.

The woman who can read subtle facial cues.
The woman who's quick witted, a fast talker.

You ignore me like I'm garbage.
I'm not pretty like other women.
I'm not thin like other women.
I'm not athletic like other women.

I'm a retarded fat freak nobody wants.
Not even my own father wanted me.

He left me when I was 3 – you can't
see past my face, my true personality.

You can't see my true mind and thoughts.
Nobody does – nobody gives me a chance.

Nobody wants to get to know me better
as a person – nobody wants to

get past my outer mask to know me.
I have feelings, you know, I'm intelligent,

smart and I have interests of worth.
I read widely. I have an English degree

Silent Meow by T.K. Torme

but because you refuse to ask me out
for coffee you will never ever get to know

the real me and get to peel
back my outer mask.

You lose out on getting to know
an awesome person.

Silent Meow by T.K. Torme

Crows

Crows taught
Phantom a very
valuable lesson when
she was still a kitten.

She brought home
a dead baby crow
that she caught
by herself. Proud
of her prize, 'til
she left the kitchen
to go into the yard
for fresh air.

For two summers
crows dive bombed
her mercilessly
each time she dared
to go out. So back
inside she retreated
to safety from the
birds of menace to
her own world.

Since that time she would
not hunt another
living creature again;
only dead leaves.

Silent Meow by T.K. Torme

The crows taught
her one life rule
she lived by 'til death:
DO NOT FUCK WITH CROWS.

Silent Meow by T.K. Torme

Épouse Inconnue

You're scattered throughout
my family tree
like sprinkles on
cupcakes. The Gosselins
and Chouinards in
Québec have kept
careful records of
our family with names
and dates – except for you.

You remain that
cold case mystery
where I wonder just
who were you. Were
you one of our First
Nation's ancestors who
lived in Québec?

How do I identify myself?
Am I French Canadian,
Métis or Indigenous?
Or am I a person with
Indigenous roots in
Canada who is also
French Canadian?

I do not wish to claim
ghosts that do not

Silent Meow by T.K. Torme

belong to me. Yet I
I wish to honor all
ghosts who have walked
before me – who are part
of my blood and bones.

Silent Meow by T.K. Torme
Story In A Dozen Haiku

I have a story
and it deserves to be told.
I need to be heard.

God, please, please help me.
Fix my disabilities.
Heal me. Make me whole.

Nothing is just an
accident. God has his say
in your destiny.

Insulting others
brings out hatred, bitterness,
sadness and despair.

Ev'ry single day:
Focus on the happiness.
Ignore the despair.

Life is far too short
to dwell on petty grudges.
They just drain the soul.

My pain is hidden
to the naked eye, but I
suffer every day.

Silent Meow by T.K. Torme

Pain envelops me,
consumes all my energy,
leaves me exhausted.

I must mask myself,
pretend ev'rything's alright,
while I fall apart.

I'm the family freak
where I don't belong because
I have Asperger's.

The bonus of cats
is they will not ever bark.
Cats do rule the world.

You keep chiding me,
'Why don't you go kill yourself?'
Well, maybe I will.

Silent Meow by T.K. Torme

Haunted

You've silently become
a ghost in the wind.

I could not fly to see
you one last time
because of the COVID
Pandemic – restrictions.

Yet I am still haunted
by you – your voice,
hear you – as if you
are still here, alive.

but you are not –
only a ghost – a
whisper, a thought –
but I'm still brought
back to all the times
we spent together
as family – holidays
your warm smile
I can never forget.
Silenced forever.

Haunted always by you.
I'm sorry for all the
hurt I've caused you.
I hope you've forgiven me.

Hell

My hell runs deep
and wide as an ocean.

Past words and taunting
from years ago still run
in my mind like a broken record.

I replay each and every single
horrible memory over and over again –
a Chinese water torture.
My mind self-torturing.
I carry an Elephant's memory –

All grudges run long and
deep. All those who
have done me wrong I
remember with hatred and
the bitterness of a peppercorn.

Every single day my heart
screams in despair.
The whispers and memories
where my tragic masquerade
plays out flowing tears of acid.

Silent Meow by T.K. Torme
I Am 1

I am
peace, love and warmth.
I like reading books and watching musicals.
Trust, friendship, and faith are important to me.
I really enjoy being useful.
I can be obstinate when I receive help.
But I am grateful when I receive it.
I love animals.
I feel strongly about peace.
I believe in education.
This is me. I am!

I Am 2

I am
shy, ambitious, and studious.
I like the world of literature and the world of theatre.
Sensitivity, warmth and caring are important to me.
I really enjoy solitary peace.
I can be fearsome when my pride is hurt.
But I make sure I am sensitive to other people's feelings.
I love cats.
I feel strongly about Literature.
I believe in education.
This is me.
I am!

Silent Meow by T.K. Torme

Indiana Jones

Back during the
Good Old Salad Days
Of Montreal we were
carefree children –
innocent in the world
of adult matters.

One cold winter's day we went to
see an *Indiana Jones*
movie at Cinema V.

We went to Steinberg's
to buy a 2 L bottle of coke
you stashed under your
thick coat. I watched
in astonishment as you coolly paid
for your movie ticket
walked to the concession
to ask for two cups for
us to share our beverage
during the movie.

That day is now but
a ghost in my memory
which I fondly remember
during the Good Old
Salad Days Of Montreal.
Do you remember too?

Silent Meow by T.K. Torme

Inspiration

Inspiration feeds the mind.
Inspiration feeds the soul.
I stitch all day long just to unwind.
I read and write to feel whole.

Poetry soothes my inner self.
Prose feeds my imagination.
Needlework sits upon my bookshelf.
Threads, floss, fabric bring me
to a whole new station.

One needs a creative outlet
to express oneself.
You need paint, paper, fabric
to say who you really are.
Without an outlet you sit on a lofty shelf.

One needs a place to become
their own solo star.

Journal

My first journal:
to write in,
record thoughts
and events

My own solace.
Private world.
just for me
while I am
just a ghost
in this world
all alone.

Salad Days.
Montreal.
Childhood.

Silent Meow by T.K. Torme

KGB

It's Monday morning
in the middle of the year.
Mr. Barta's crying.
He tells us the KGB
came to our school,
dressed in business suits,
whisked one of our classmates
back to Russia. It was
quick; sudden – flash – surprise.
He understands the KGB.
He came from Hungary
where this also happened.

I'm sad my classmate's gone.
I still do not understand.
The reality that came
close to my face
is still a foreign concept
of a far away.
This is Canada.
It does not happen here.
Nothing of value or
importance ever happens
in Canada.

I grow up.
I still think of that
Monday morning and

Silent Meow by T.K. Torme

Mr. Barta – the KGB
who whisked one of my
classmates back to Russia.
Their whispers and echoes
still resonate in my
inner core to this very day.

The KGB lives on.
I wonder ... what happened
to my classmate?

Silent Meow by T.K. Torme

Kindle

Back during the Salad Days
my cats Phantom and Opera had kittens
between 1993-1996.

Batches and batches of cute,
fluffy kindles of kittens
who took hostage of my bed where
they were born and slept there.

I surrendered my bed to them
to raise their families
while I camped out on
the living room couch.

Phantom once
gave birth right
next to my face
while I slept soundly
waking up to the
mewing of tiny
newborn kittens
blind to the world.

Those were the Good
Old Salad Days.

Phantom and Opera
have, long ago, become ghosts.

Silent Meow by T.K. Torme

Leonard Cohen

You and I-
have a commonality:
We stalked the same Noble Halls
of our school, Roslyn Elementary.

We cut our teeth on the playground;
learned in the very same rooms.

You walked your path decades before;
leaving an electrical energy behind.

I felt your presence when I roamed
the Halls before I knew you went there.
I only knew an energy;
A silent presence
your lingering energy
encouraged me to write
poetry and stories.

During my personal years
in a private hell, you
Whispered in my ear,
"Hang in there – everything's
going to be fine."

My writing was my salvation
to my own private war I battled
every single day.

Silent Meow by T.K. Torme

No one knew my
secret torment:
Constant sadness
I could not shake;
anger as horrible
as the Holocaust;
self-loathing and
hatred; daily grief
of my father leaving
me at age three.

Deep down I felt
I must have been a
horrible person – to
be unwanted and unloved
by my own father.

When I grew up,
I learned of your existence.
I was proud we both
lived in Westmount.

When you died,
I was sad. You were
no longer able to
Inspire others with
new poetry.

But your energy
always be felt by me.

Silent Meow by T.K. Torme

List Poem

Birth
Baby
Child
Carefree
Love
Toy
Teddy Bear
Hobby
Growth
Teenager
Puberty
Maturity
Job
Adulthood
Responsibilities
Money
House
Marriage
Children
Grandparent
Old Age
Disease
Widowed
Death

Silent Meow by T.K. Torme

Loss

I look for you
everywhere
after you left me
when i was three.

My heart screamed
while I cried bitter tears.

Classmates
and teachers
taunted me,

Words masked under
sweet false honey smiles –

Hidden messages,
spewed venom;
and now I'm left alone
to chase away
dream ghosts.

Silent Meow by T.K. Torme
Pink Bunnies

Way back during The Salad Days Of Montreal
I walked the Noble Halls of Roslyn Elementary.
I was in your French Immersion class where
you taught French and Mrs. Glover taught English.

I clung to you – hung around you for company –
I craved human contact. But you did not like me.
I puzzled – why did you not like me?
Was I not a likeable person?
In art we drew bunnies and I drew pink bunnies
because I loved the color pink (and still do).
Little did I excpect your wrath, anger.
You sent me to the principal's office
for this mortal sin – a grave offence in your eyes.
I did not know what I did wrong –
Yet my mother was called in from work
over my "offence".

You were crying because I drew pink bunnies.
You insisted pink bunnies did not exist –

What a traumatic event in my life –
shattering a love of art, confidence in my abilities.
I still doubt my talent in art.
And I'm still
chasing away those dream ghosts –
that chased me away
back in the Salad Days of Montreal.

Silent Meow by T.K. Torme

Salad Days

Back during the
Salad Days of Montreal:
Snowstorms,
Trick or treating,
Innocence,
Loss of belongings,
Year of Hell. –

I was a child
in my own world –
doing my own thing:
Writing poetry.
Chasing away
'Dream Ghosts'.

Those were the
Good Old Salad Days
Of Montreal.

Silent Meow by T.K. Torme

Seagulls

How odd it seems to see them perched
upon a lamppost looking down on us.
In my head, for the answer,
I've searched and searched
even on the way to my classes
on the bus.

The only answer I came up with is this.
They like lampposts - it's their perch
from above in daytime-
just like a bat at night.

They are silent as a Birch tree,
yet they clamor for our food
when we walk by them at Stanley Park.

Is it any wonder when
women, children, and men
have hot dogs to eat,
there are many seagulls
ready to take them from you?

If you don't share,
they will stick to you like glue.

Silent Meow by T.K. Torme

Sisters

Do you remember
The Good Old Salad Days of Montreal –
where we walked the Noble Halls
of Roslyn Elementary?

We were only children then
wanting a sibling for ourselves.
We told all the teachers
we were sisters – they believed us –
We were convincing.
until a parent teacher meeting –

Our mothers were confronted
with this story –
teachers were puzzled.
How we were related –
a yarn that needed untangling.

But what a great memory
I cherish from the
Good old Salad Days Of Montreal.

Do you Remember too?

Silent Meow by T.K. Torme
Battle Of The Brians

Calgary 1988.
Winter Olympics.
Cold War.
Russia, KGB.

The Battle of the Brians.
Orser VS Boitano.
Canada vs the USA.
Who will reign Supreme?

The Battle For Gold:
Olympic Champion

On ice – two greats
skate for their lives

to win the Olympics
Masked in rivalry:

Mental Battle for
a clean skate.

Boitano glides on
Ice – the crowd roars.

Orser – Flag bearer
For Opening Ceremony,

Silent Meow by T.K. Torme

Battles for clean skate,
Trips – but captures hearts,

Worldwide. Boitano
wins gold. Orser

wins silver. Two different
Destinies emerge: Masked
Under epic Olympic
battle – Orser rises to
fame as skating
coach – Olympic medalists

from worldwide. His
destiny meant to glide

under this path of twirls
and jumps. Would he

have gone this route if
he had won gold? A humble

silver opens more paths
than a gold. Humility

teaches more than a
clear victory. The battle

of the Brians – forever
the great skate battle of all time!

Silent Meow by T.K. Torme

The Seashore

I walk the seashore
Of Burrard inlet
which is part of the Pacific Ocean.

It is a beautiful day in May.
I go barefoot.
I see seashells.
Wait,-there is something moving!

There is a crab-so tiny!
I pick it up and examine it
then I put him down.

I go to a fish and chips place
I have Halibut and chips.
The best!

I go home and have supper
Amanda, I wish you
a happy first communion
from your cousin, Tara

**This poem was written on Monday May 4, 1992.
The first communion of my cousin Amanda
took place in Toronto on May 3, 1992,
the day I went to the beach.**

Silent Meow by T.K. Torme

Tiger

Stripes, stripes everywhere! See them in
all sizes, and degrees of fear. Watch as
they run, hide, stalk, pounce and win
over their prey.

How majestic, rhythmic like jazz.
So elegant in their beautiful fur coats,
so graceful like a ballerina on the stage.-
Yet solitary to the degree
of being on the go all the time
to hide away from us.

I'd make a wager
on the whole endangered species.
They'll survive.

Somehow-Nature always thrives.
It's a fact of life.
As insects of a solitary hive,
they rear their young with such a knack.

These beautiful creatures-
slaughtered to death
may soon be extinct
in a very short breath.

Silent Meow by T.K. Torme

Unmasked

We meet you and I.
A connection between us.
Sparks fly.
Common interests;
Common background;
Common roots.

We play a dance : Words mask
what we really desire.
We take it really slow,
play games unmasking our
layers slowly _onion peel
getting to the root of what we
really desire:

Coming to our passions
You and I : Lips locked tingled
Unmasking our naked selves
Skin on skin; flesh on flesh;
A bond growing stronger
with each meeting.

Past hurts slowly dissolving
into a pool of liquid vapor
Turning fear into feed.

Learning to
rock the mask.

Silent Meow by T.K. Torme
Weeping Willow

You're the subject of my dreams.
Your branches reach out like moonbeams

You cover my weeping tears.
You nurture my dreams – not fears.

Your branches soothe my pain
I wonder: *"Will I get well again?"*

Is it possible to feel this way,
and be a million miles away?

Your bark: medicine for me.
Your touch helps me to just be.

Can you soothe my aching soul
and help me to be more whole?

Silent Meow by T.K. Torme

When I Die

When I die I want to be
washed in a large washing
machine through several
rinse cycles and lots
of detergents –
then tumble dry
for a long time before
I walk up to the Pearly
Gates to St. Peter and
then God to be judged for
what I've done.

Let me be questioned by God
so I can atone for my actions –
to be Chrysler Building shiny.

Silent Meow by T.K. Torme

Wild Cat

I'm a cat and I'm wild.
I do not belong to man, woman or child.
Roaming in the woods makes me purr
but not when someone tries to flatten my fur!
Oh the life is-to catch birds and mice.
An occasional tidbit from a house is nice!
The woods, the hills, the valleys I roam.
The whole wide world is my home!

**This poem was originally written in 1988
when I was in Grade 5 for a school assignment.**

Silent Meow by T.K. Torme

Wonder

What happened
to you when
the KGB whisked
your entire family
back to Russia?

I was just a child in
Mr. Barta's Grade Five
Class at Roslyn Elementary.
He cried over the news
of your demise.
I sat there, confused,
stunned, devoid of anything.
The shock quietly crept in,
and for decades I slowly
processed what happened.
Where did you go?
What did you do with your life?

In the wake of today's
world events I am haunted
by your shadow –
the KGB that silently
Crept up into my own world –
a cactus of events
and I want to ask you:

Are you ok?

Silent Meow by T.K. Torme

Graveyard

In Tadoussac my mother took me
to visit a cute, small graveyard.
It was sprinkled with
the ghosts and bones of those
who lived long ago. Maybe some
might have been my ancestors.
Young children
Haunted this graveyard.

I ponder decades later:
What happened in the lives
Of those now slumbering
for eternity? What illness
cut their lives so short?

Silent Meow by T.K. Torme
Whale Watching

Before we left for Montreal
we went on a whale watching
tour in Tadoussac.

It rained and poured that morning
wrapped in a veil of mist and fog.

In my yellow rain suit I shivered
while drinking hot chocolate.

We saw no whales but
lots of fog and rain that day.

The boat came back to dock
and I changed out of the rain suit.

It cleared up
when we left for Montreal.

Silent Meow by T.K. Torme
Roslyn Choir

At Roslyn I was in Senior Choir.
On Tuesdays and Thursdays
we practiced with Mme. Gagne
and Mme. Bryant. Vocal
Exercises I still remember.

Concerts all over the city
Including the P.S.B.G.M. –
Learning to say *Merde*
before a concert for good
luck – learning new
songs to sing.

And now
I wonder what happened
to my two choir teachers.

Ugunskurs

At Saulaine we sat 'round
The Ugunskurs, singing songs,
making smores and
banana boats. Our songs
were all in Latvian while
we connected to each other
in the dusky evening.
Young children to older children
enjoying an evening out
from our sleeping quarters
for a memorable time
with the counselors back
during the Good Old Salad Days.

Silent Meow by T.K. Torme

Corner Talk

My mother and I needed
a new place to live
and time was running short.
After several fruitless searches
we found a place perfect for us.
The landlord, Anne, was hesitant
while my mother talked.

Anne backed away while
my mother slowly advanced
while she talked – literally
backing Anne into a corner.

I was finally given a clear example
of what talking someone
into a corner looks like.

Silent Meow by T.K. Torme

November Sonnet

It's raining today.
Here comes November.
Turn the sun away.
Let me remember:
All the warmth of June.
Swimming in the pool.
Watch the summer moon.
Time for Christmas Yule.
Mass on Christmas Eve.
Light the Christmas tree.
Find what you believe.
Let everything be.
The end of the year
is quite nearly here.

Silent Meow by T.K. Torme

Walking Stick

I went mushroom picking
with Oma and Opa in Ontario
for orange colored mushrooms
what Oma would make into a yummy
creamy sauce we'd all eat
when camping. We found a
stick that Opa had taken
to carve my name on it just
for me with ends for
ready walking. That stick
was all mine. I used it
when visiting them in Toronto.
Since then the stick has
travelled back with me to
Vancouver – where it rests in
my closet covered with cobwebs
ready for another memory
with someone else while
I remember Oma and Opa
who are no longer here.

I wish I knew how much
they really meant to me
when they were alive.

Silent Meow by T.K. Torme
Father's Day 1991

My father was briefly
"found" by Uncle Jean-Luc.

A family reunion with him –
was only for family – but not me.

An arrangement
to meet him at the Days Inn
for Father's Day where
I waited for hours.

He never showed up.
I tornadoed to my room
in anger and tears.

That year I received
'the one and only'
birthday card from him
with the inscription:

"From a distance, as a father,
I have always loved you."

Silent Meow by T.K. Torme

Annie

My mother took me to see
"Annie" when I was a child.
It starred Carol Burnett and
Albert Finney.

There was a short intermission
to change the reels. I fell in love with
the movie and I played the record daily
'til I had nearly memorized
the entire record. A neighbor
got sick and tired of my record,
climbed into our window
and turned it off.

Silent Meow by T.K. Torme

Wasaga Beach

I played backgammon with you
in Toronto as a child.
Those summer days
at Wasaga Beach amongst
the stalking seagulls
were eager for food.

We took turns all three of us
in playing and you instructing
me the automatic moves
one makes for a better outcome
of the game.

>And now
>your battered,
>worn out game
>is mine.

Silent Meow by T.K. Torme

Reward

I saw an old lady
one Sunday in the alleyway
near my house attacking
a mother raccoon
and her babies.

I yelled at her to STOP –
I didn't like her hurting them.

The mother raccoon
let her babies come up to
my feet for a sniff.

And then I went on home.

When I went back out again
that same day
I found two $20 bills -
cash on the street.

Silent Meow by T.K. Torme

Pensionnaire

I boarded at
Academie Michele Provost
in grade two.
I had a room with a view
of the schoolyard.

The hours of French homework
piled up while we worked
on our Assignments.

Weekly Movie Nights
with my classmates
and breakfast and supper
at the school –

My favorite
No. 27 glass for milk
with Brussel Sprouts --
and uniforms
to wear every day.

Silent Meow by T.K. Torme

Grade One

I looked forward to my first day
of Grade One at Academie Michele Provost.
My mother and I went to a special
store for my school supplies
and my uniform.

I was excited
to go to school
and learn.

I packed all my Dr Seuss books
in my bag for my first day.

My mother quietly explained
to me what we'd be learning.

And my school bag was repacked.

Silent Meow by T.K. Torme

Pink Boots

My obsession with pink
came to a climax in grade four
that winter my mother
and I went shopping for
winter boots.

There were lots of nice boots
but they all hurt my feet
as they were not pink.

I could not settle.
Finally we found Duckies
for the cold, snowy
Montreal weather.

They were pink.
They fit me well.

    And, sadly,
it did not snow that winter.

Silent Meow by T.K. Torme
MacDoherty's

MacDoherty's was an ice-cream shop
in Westmount. An old-fashioned store
with the best ice-cream and sprinkles
for the residents who haunted that shop.

After a play at Westmount Hall
we would walk over for ice-cream
with sprinkles and a waffle cone
of yummy deliciousness;
then the comfort of a campfire
with Smores on a cone.

Silent Meow by T.K. Torme
English Class

At Westmount High School
Mrs. Macaulay had "accidentally"
put me into Mr. Bracegirdle's
Advance English in grade 8.
A class where I flourished
and loved the writing projects.

It was my happy place until
I got transferred to the
regular class of unruly students
and a teacher whom I saw
throw a chair at a student –

    Unforgettable!

Silent Meow by T.K. Torme
Westmount Library

I almost lived at Westmount Library
where I went nearly
Every single weekday.
The Library was betwixt
Westmount Hall
and the greenhouse
with a corridor connecting
all three like a secret passage.

It was a quiet space where
I could squirrel myself away
into the safety of words
and books of writers
that calmed my anxiety
and depression back during
The Good Old Salad Days.

Silent Meow by T.K. Torme
Yann Hradecky

A few days before me
11th birthday in Deaumaine
Deauville I met Yann Hradecky
at the pool.

He slid down the slide –
I gathered up the courage
To talk to him.

We struck up a fast friendship
Hanging out together,
Playing, having adventures
In the country.

When I moved to Vancouver, BC –
I never saw him again.

Silent Meow by T.K. Torme

Leo

My Leo started off as a
Full stuffed toy with head
And arms and legs
And a full body.

Then it dwindled town
To just a head worn out, sewn up
Until one day in grade four
I brought him to school in
My pocked where he just
Disappeared in the school
Yard at lunch.

I went back
After lunch with a teacher –
To find him gone forever.

Silent Meow by T.K. Torme

T K Torme Bio

T K Torme was born Tara Kimberley Torme in Montreal, Quebec in 1977 and moved to Vancouver, BC in 1992. She received her B.A. in English in 2001. T K has been writing since she was a child and has always loved reading and writing poetry. It brings her great joy & relaxation and opens her mind to new possibilities allowing her to expand her thoughts and channel them from her mind to the page into poetry.

T K has Asperger's Syndrome, and she finds poetry helps her to express her feelings with vision and clarity in concise words.

www.ingramcontent.com/pod-product-compliance
Lightning Source LLC
Chambersburg PA
CBHW052146070526
44585CB00017B/2004